Katrin Trautwein

WORKING WITH COLOR

Library of 400 Combinations

Birkhäuser
Basel

Katrin Trautwein

INTRODUCTION

Selecting the most beautiful and functional color combinations to complement flooring, architectural design, and client preferences is a complex challenge. How can one anticipate whether a combination will appear outdated or faded within just a few years? The prevalence of all-white architecture often reflects an attempt to bypass this dilemma. However, such designs frequently result in excessive light reflection on a purely functional level, while also reinforcing an unfortunate bias that equates whiteness with neutrality and superiority.

This color library serves as a practical tool, offering 400 balanced color combinations designed to harmonize with any architectural style. After selecting the main color in a concept—most often a shade of white or the color of the flooring—designers and clients can choose from a family of ten suitable combinations to form their preferred palette.

The colors featured in this book are the result of 25 years of research dedicated to analyzing samples from historic sites and iconic buildings designed by visionaries such as Le Corbusier, Eileen Gray, the Bauhaus artists of Dessau, Bruno Taut, Lux Guyer, Verner Panton, and Hans Scharoun. kt.COLOR, the artisan paint company I founded, has developed a palette of 225 architecturally useful colors rooted in a deep respect for natural pigments. The palette reflects a broad spectrum of architectural philosophies on beauty.

The prints in this book are high-quality CMYK reproductions of 159 of these paint colors. Several whites are included, as white is the most important color in most concepts. However, only whites darker than the color of the paper could be printed. By using chlorine-free, natural paper, we were able to include French White (which is identical in tone to the paper) as a default main color for the concepts.

While the color prints on this paper provide an excellent starting point for color consultations, they cannot fully convey the richness, depth, spatial effect, and tactile appeal of the original pigments. Final color selections should always be made using authentic color samples crafted from the appropriate pigments. Such samples can be ordered online at ktcolor.com, with details available in the index at the back of the book.

HOW TO USE THIS COLOR LIBRARY

Each of the 400 combinations consists of:

1. The default white of the natural paper, which corresponds to French White.
2. The color of the flooring or a darker white, in cases where French White is too bright for the concept.
3. A deeper achromatic color, typically a natural gray.
4. Two additional complementary colors, including a range of chromatic colors and several blacks.

French White may be the main color used for walls and ceilings in combination with a flooring color, or it may be the trim color to be combined with a darker white. Each darker white or flooring color is shown with ten different concepts. While flipping through the pages can offer inspiration, I recommend starting with the main color—either your preferred white, or a shade closest to the flooring. These colors dictate the structure of the book and are placed at the bottom of each page. Ten concepts are dedicated to each of these main colors. The main colors, from the lightest printable white to Anthracite, are shown on the table of contents inside the cover flaps. The final color concepts represent wood tones, from very light ochre to dark stained woods. These concepts are just as useful for wood constructions as they are for wood flooring.

The underlying logic of these selections is based on my research into the multi-faceted relationships between light, color, emotions, spatial navigation, and perception. This color library was created for designers and homeowners who wish to apply the principles of spatial perception to their projects effectively—without having to study the theory.

This book owes its existence to the colors created by the talented kt.COLOR team. Its beautiful design was created by Lena Mahr. Katharina Kulke, my editor, Angelika Gaal, production at Birkhäuser publishers, and my husband Klaus contributed valuable insights and corrections. I extend my deepest gratitude to all of you. Creating this book was a pleasure, and I hope that its good spirit inspires those who use it.

Katrin Trautwein

CHAMPAGNE WHITE

08KT001

18KT021

18KT017

17KT004

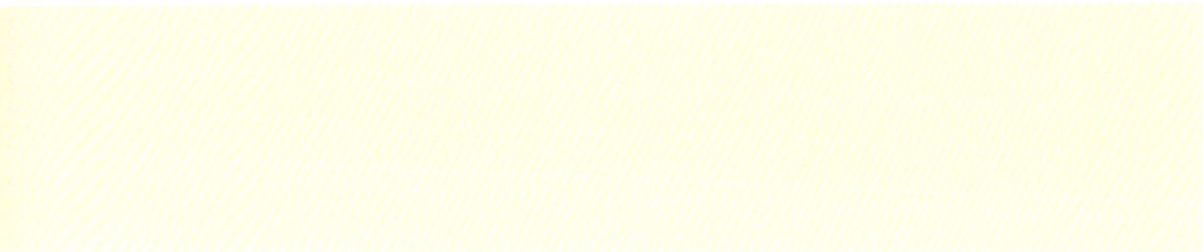

08KT001

26KT071

18KT027

23KT114

08KT001

32KT010

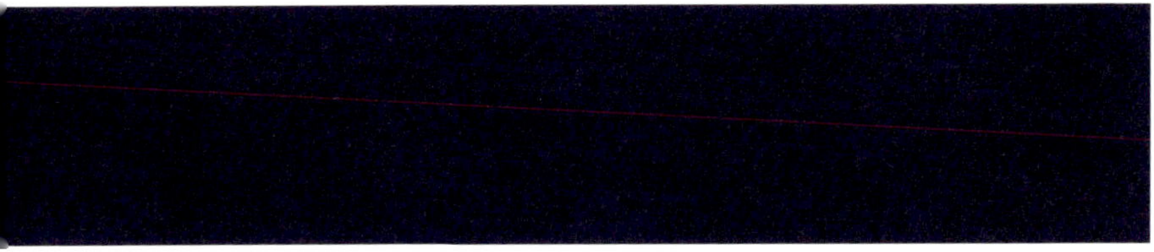

11KT020

15KT057

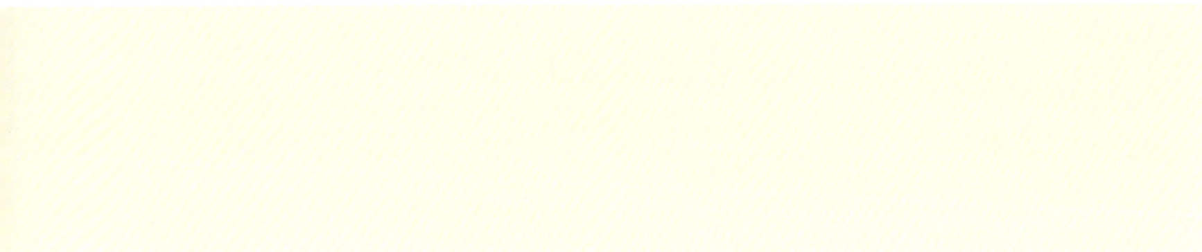

08KT001

32KT041

08KT007

08KT013

08KT001

17KT060

43KT22

32KT033

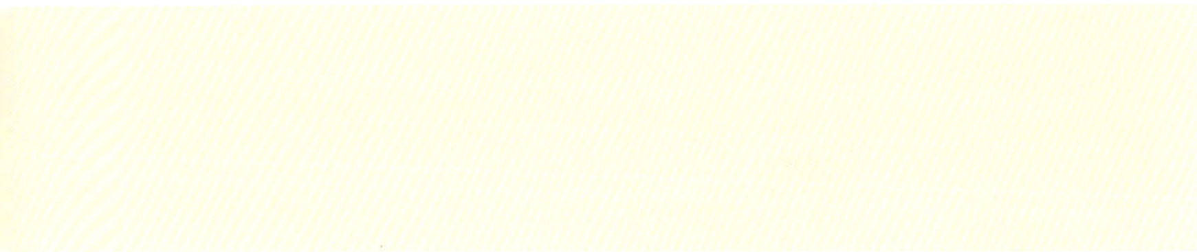

08KT001

08KT022

22KT021

16KT002

08KT001

08KT044

43KT17

16KT006

08KT001

21KT007

07KT055

10KT010

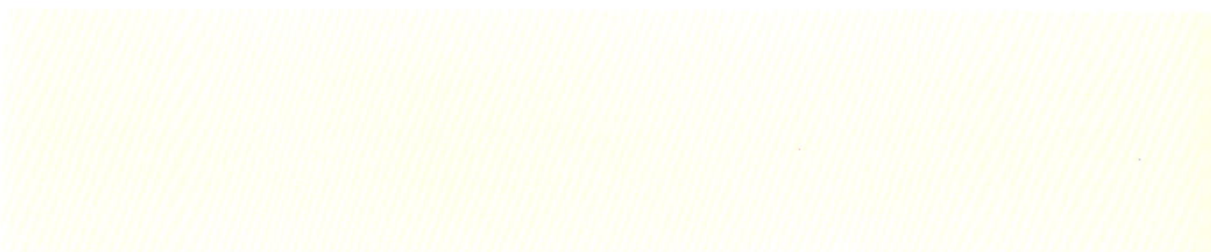

08KT001

17KT036

20KT305

26KT013

08KT001

11KT020

32KT110

11KT054

08KT001

WARM NATURAL WHITE

12KT099

26KT013

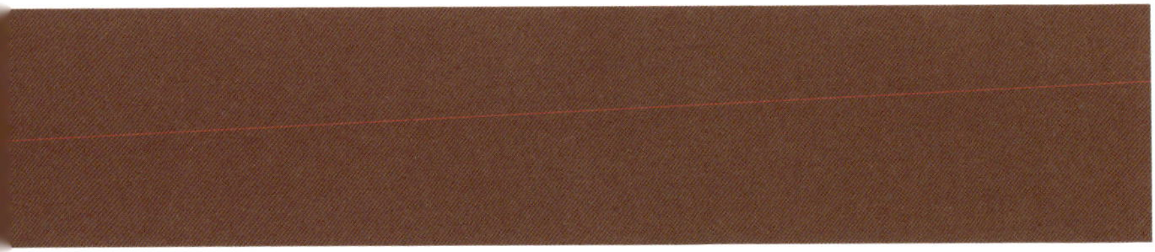

43KT04

11KT020

12KT099

08KT044

12KT001

26KT013

12KT099

16KT061

24KT094

32KT143

12KT099

08KT005

20KT318

22KT034

12KT099

21KT003

08KT009

26KT013

12KT099

26KT013

24KT040

25KT001

12KT099

24KT091

22KT021

10KT003

12KT099

12KT050

43KT26

32KT023

12KT099

18KT017

32KT131

21KT011

12KT099

04KT003

43KT06

26KT013

12KT099

SHALE WHITE

32KT006

07KT015

26KT046

14KT003

32KT006

21KT010

21KT005

06KT001

32KT006

24KT020

43KT04

32KT034

32KT006

32KT012

23KT114

21KT013

32KT006

24KT094

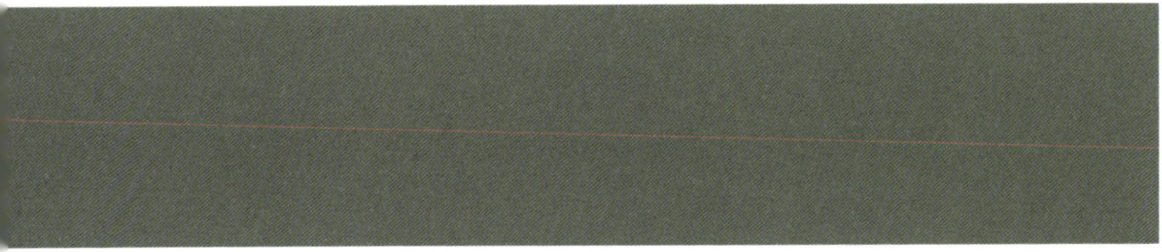

18KT020

18KT028

32KT006

32KT013

12KT044

21KT010

32KT006

17KT060

11KT120

21KT011

32KT006

21KT002

32KT032

11KT114

32KT006

23KT020

18KT016

43KT05

32KT006

43KT09

18KT027

11KT115

32KT006

IVORY WHITE

43KT02

08KT007

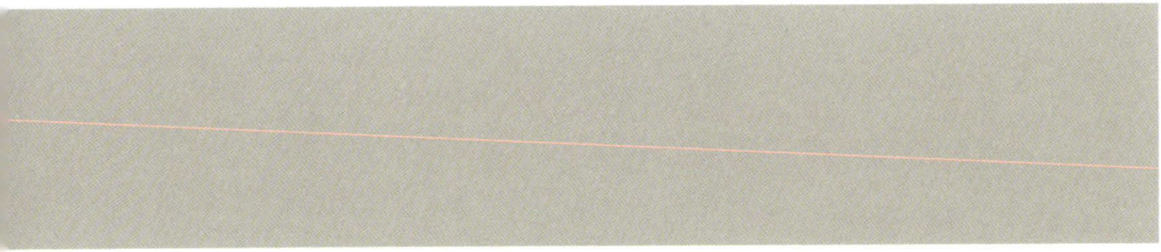

16KT002

21KT013

43KT02

12KT043

43KT26

32KT143

43KT02

32KT031

32KT033

11KT114

43KT02

06KT034

21KT006

12KT044

43KT02

32KT131

04KT004

32KT034

43KT02

18KT020

18KT014

18KT022

43KT02

07KT055

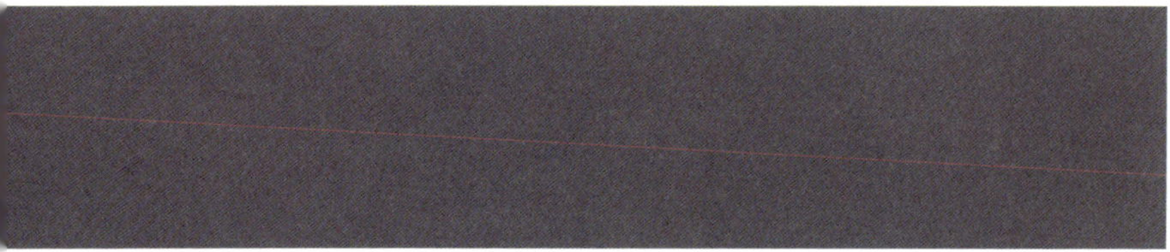

16KT061

17KT060

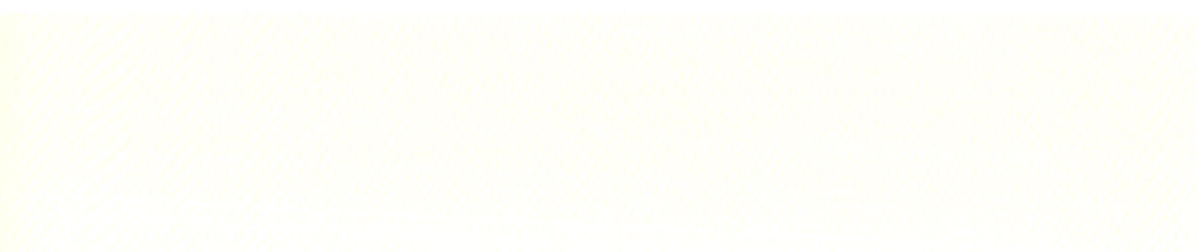

43KT02

43KT26

08KT044

21KT014

43KT02

16KT001

43KT12

15KT057

43KT02

32KT042

32KT102

10KT001

43KT02

WHISPER GRAY

26KT015

18KT016

08KT009

12KT052

26KT015

21KT011

18KT028

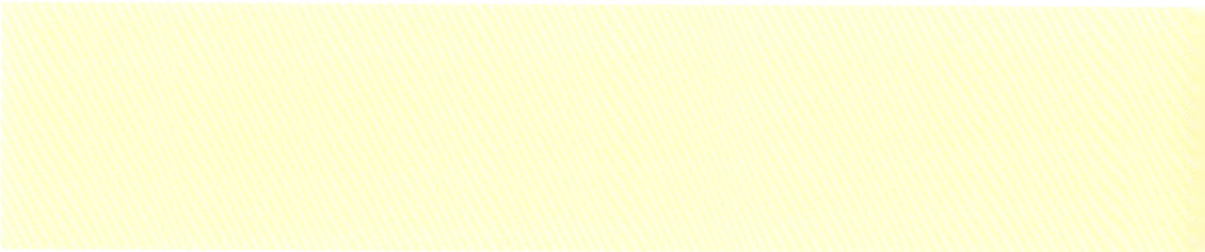

07KT056

26KT015

32KT042

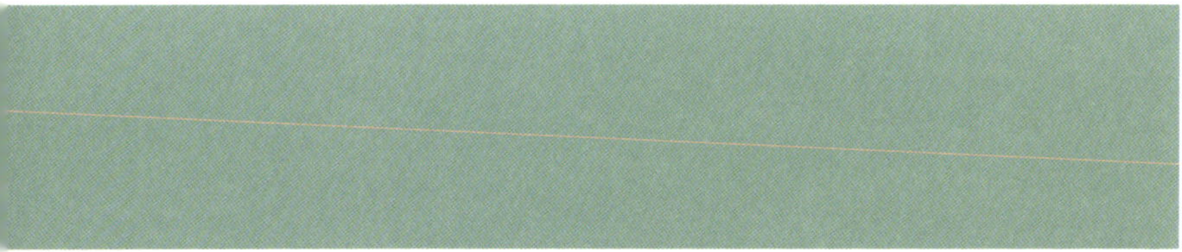

32KT041

32KT130

26KT015

15KT057

32KT023

13KT023

26KT015

24KT094

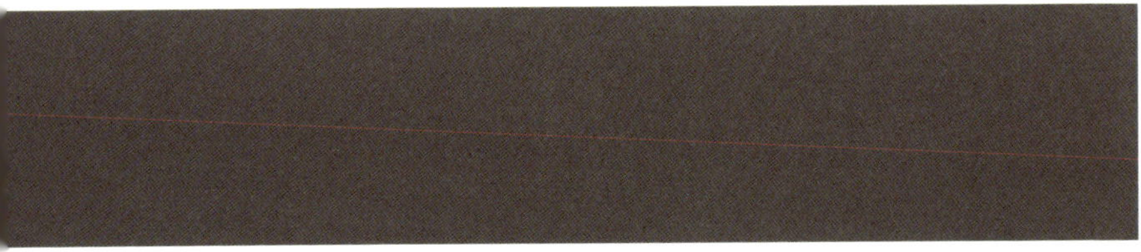

24KT050

26KT046

26KT015

18KT027

12KT121

32KT123

26KT015

43KT04

43KT16

20KT305

26KT015

32KT101

32KT041

21KT003

26KT015

11KT120

32KT043

21KT001

26KT015

22KT034

43KT23

09KT003

26KT015

NATURAL GRAY

32KT014

32KT095

21KT005

18KT021

32KT014

21KT003

26KT072

32KT042

32KT014

20KT20

24KT020

23KT114

32KT014

17KT059

24KT041

21KT002

32KT014

32KT013

11KT115

12KT048

32KT014

26KT013

20KT305

09KT024

32KT014

32KT141

43KT17

32KT042

32KT014

32KT010

17KT036

18KT021

32KT014

24KT094

18KT026

21KT009

32KT014

43KT19

12KT001

14KT003

32KT014

ROSA CASO'S WHITE

32KT007

08KT022

43KT09

32KT102

32KT007

10KT001

26KT012

32KT023

32KT007

23KT020

07KT015

32KT011

32KT007

21KT014

43KT26

32KT013

32KT007

32KT023

11KT120

32KT010

32KT007

32KT140

43KT06

21KT009

32KT007

20KT20

26KT040

32KT022

32KT007

32KT010

24KT094

32KT095

32KT007

32KT012

43KT10

06KT034

32KT007

08KT005

43KT18

08KT007

32KT007

SKY GRAY

13KT095

43KT19

43KT17

16KT006

13KT095

17KT060

43KT19

18KT022

13KT095

43KT16

26KT072

25KT001

13KT095

24KT040

23KT114

26KT046

13KT095

43KT05

32KT042

32KT141

13KT095

24KT090

10KT003

24KT094

13KT095

21KT014

08KT006

11KT114

13KT095

21KT006

32KT012

32KT013

13KT095

23KT020

18KT025

12KT044

13KT095

12KT056

32KT043

17KT060

13KT095

ZURICH WHITE

10KT075

21KT013

18KT025

16KT001

10KT075

32KT012

07KT055

32KT033

10KT075

32KT013

11KT120

32KT022

10KT075

21KT001

24KT041

21KT005

10KT075

20KT20

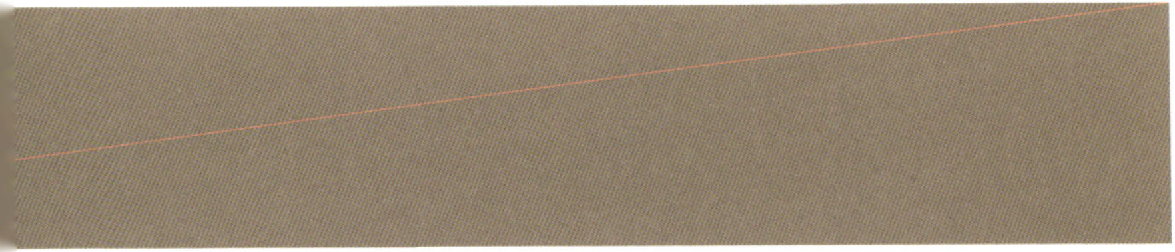

20KT318

12KT044

10KT075

26KT013

08KT009

43KT26

10KT075

43KT09

43KT06

21KT006

10KT075

16KT061

11KT114

21KT014

10KT075

16KT003

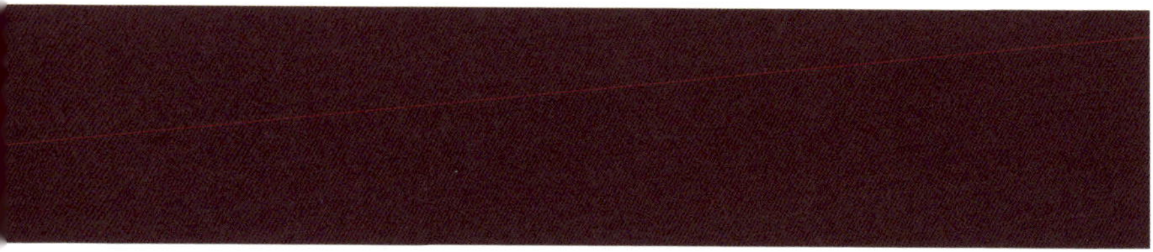

10KT001

08KT006

10KT075

16KT005

06KT034

14KT050

10KT075

SAND

24KT026

10KT003

09KT024

21KT013

24KT026

20KT318

16KT005

14KT050

24KT026

12KT001

25KT001

04KT003

24KT026

21KT010

18KT027

32KT006

24KT026

24KT094

21KT009

11KT120

24KT026

26KT072

07KT055

32KT011

24KT026

16KT002

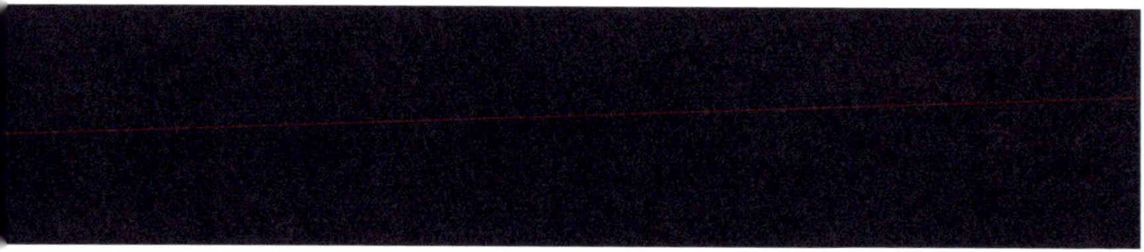

12KT048

17KT059

24KT026

21KT001

24KT091

24KT090

24KT026

21KT002

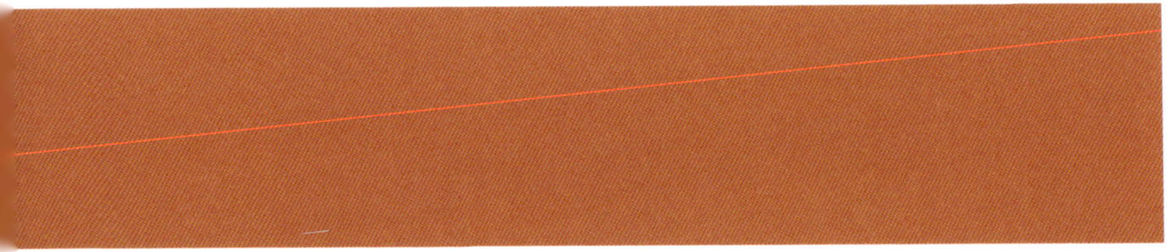

43KT23

21KT006

24KT026

43KT12

08KT044

43KT02

24KT026

FULL MOON GRAY

22KT022

16KT003

21KT012

08KT008

22KT022

12KT121

18KT026

18KT020

22KT022

22KT021

18KT016

14KT003

22KT022

10KT003

43KT04

18KT022

22KT022

24KT090

18KT014

26KT046

22KT022

12KT052

26KT072

21KT010

22KT022

32KT043

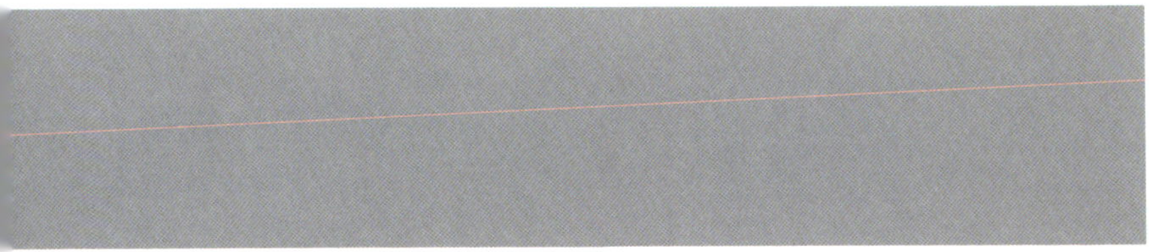

21KT009

32KT123

22KT022

16KT002

32KT042

04KT004

22KT022

32KT102

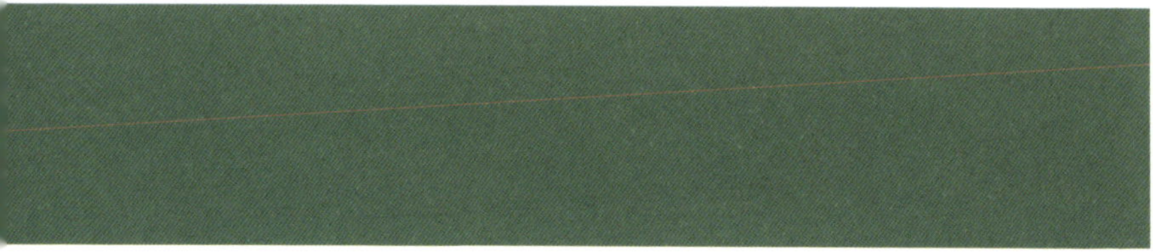

24KT041

32KT022

22KT022

32KT140

08KT008

11KT115

22KT022

LUMINOUS GRAY

20KT20

09KT002

32KT110

21KT012

20KT20

21KT012

15KT057

22KT021

20KT20

08KT044

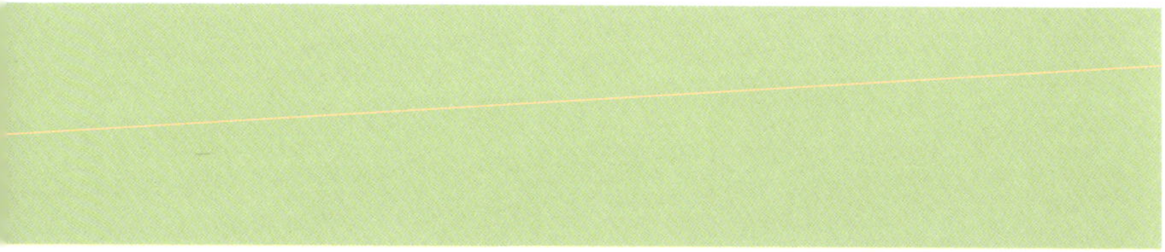

17KT059

32KT021

20KT20

32KT041

24KT041

32KT102

20KT20

13KT009

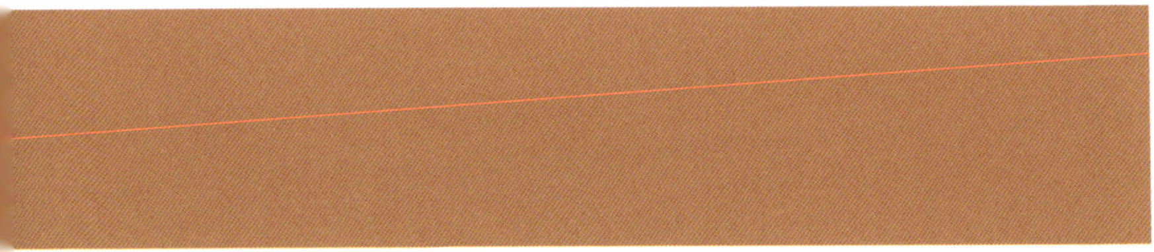

12KT121

43KT04

20KT20

32KT140

32KT100

21KT010

20KT20

32KT141

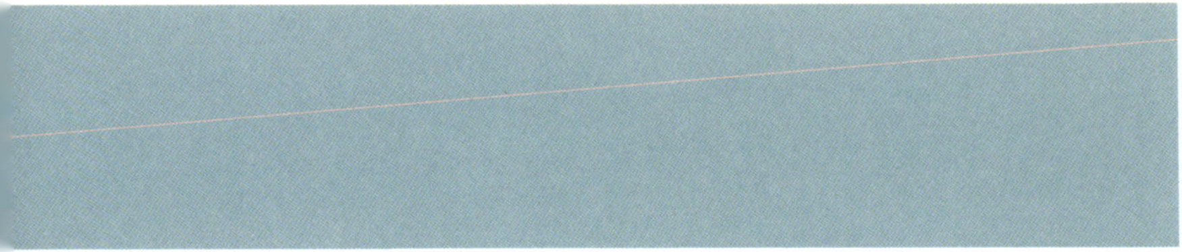

32KT032

43KT02

20KT20

32KT101

43KT17

32KT123

20KT20

32KT034

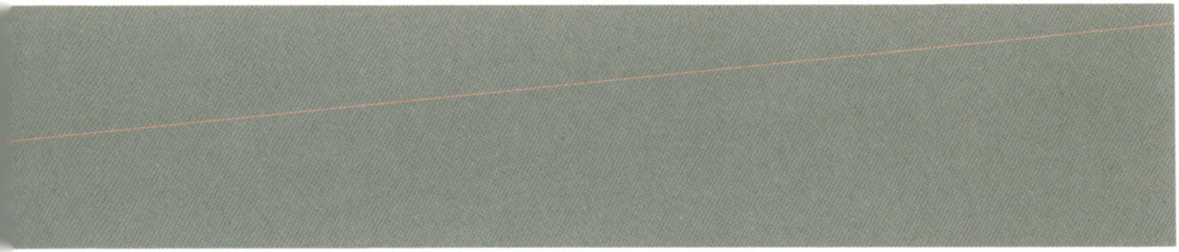

21KT012

32KT131

20KT20

32KT023

32KT090

18KT014

20KT20

MOON GRAY

16KT003

21KT005

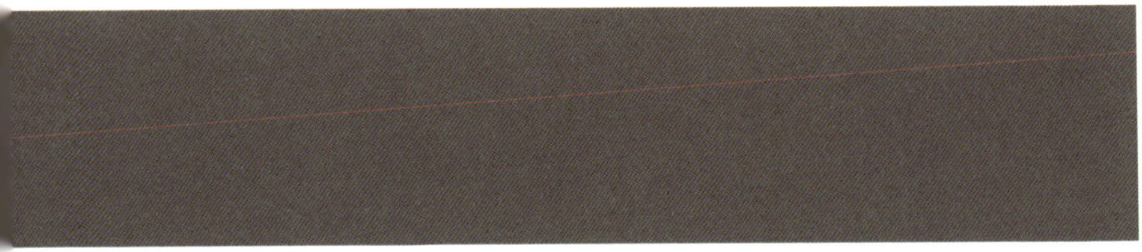

12KT056

18KT016

16KT003

21KT003

20KT318

12KT057

16KT003

12KT001

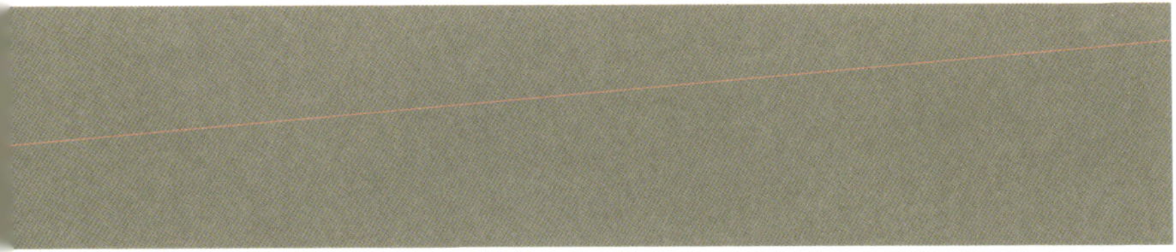

24KT020

23KT114

16KT003

11KT114

32KT140

32KT033

16KT003

11KT115

12KT044

16KT006

16KT003

11KT020

32KT102

43KT12

16KT003

15KT057

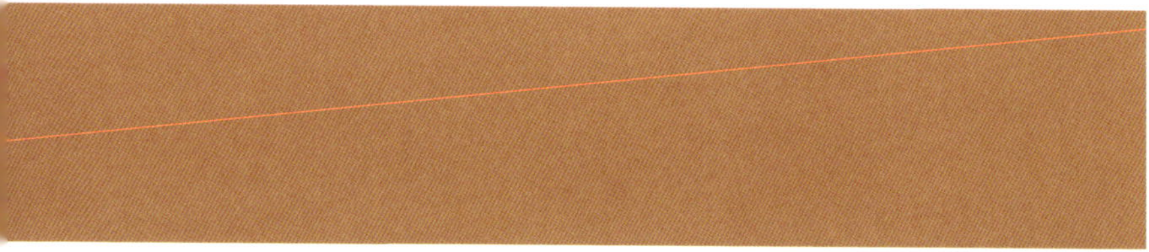

12KT121

32KT032

16KT003

18KT020

18KT022

17KT036

16KT003

43KT12

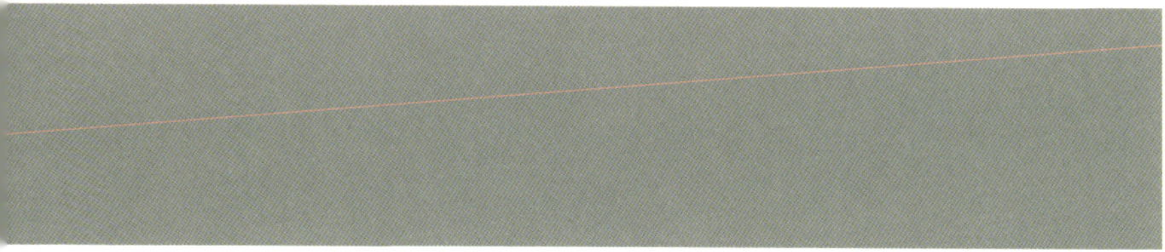

21KT012

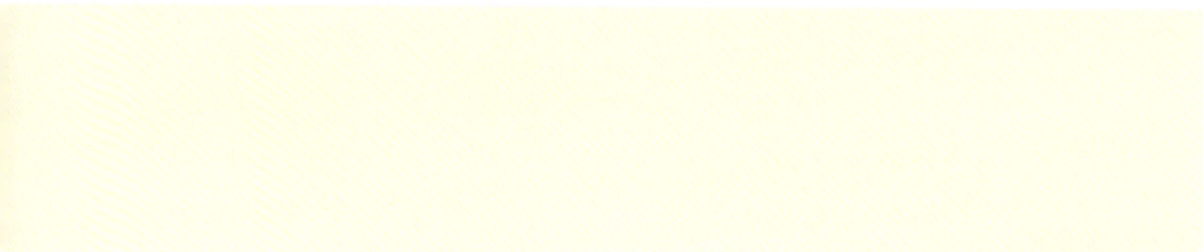

08KT001

16KT003

32KT043

04KT003

21KT002

16KT003

POLAR GRAY

23KT020

08KT022

24KT091

32KT132

23KT020

26KT040

26KT046

43KT02

23KT020

21KT013

25KT001

43KT02

23KT020

12KT121

08KT009

13KT023

23KT020

24KT020

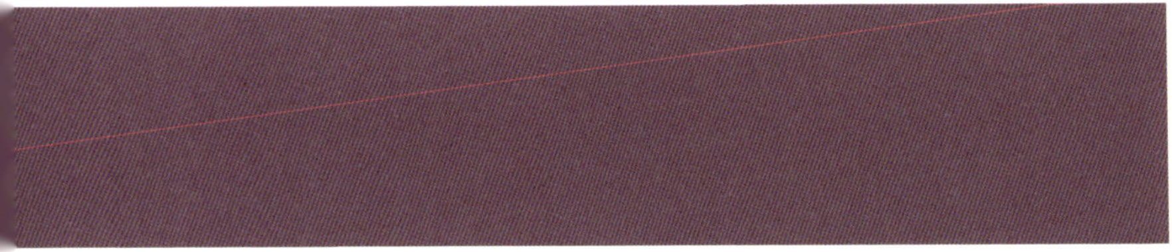

07KT055

14KT003

23KT020

07KT015

17KT059

32KT110

23KT020

12KT043

24KT094

21KT010

23KT020

43KT22

06KT001

18KT018

23KT020

43KT11

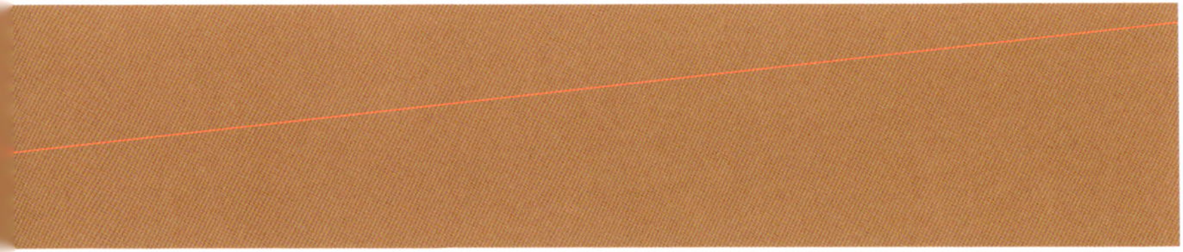

12KT121

07KT055

23KT020

43KT23

12KT056

08KT009

23KT020

GRAY VELVET

26KT013

10KT001

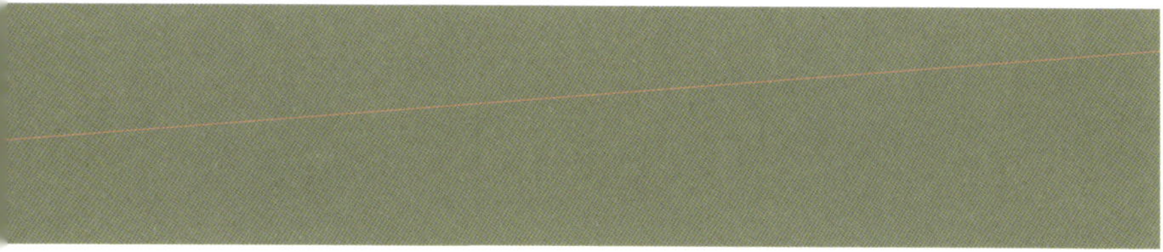

07KT015

32KT006

26KT013

08KT003

32KT140

32KT110

26KT013

43KT26

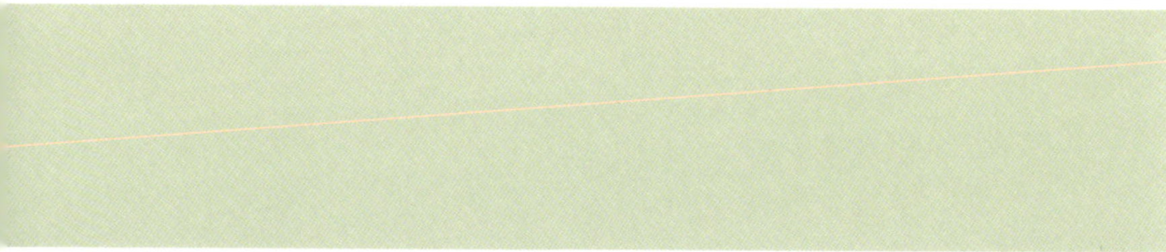

32KT043

32KT010

26KT013

14KT050

32KT029

21KT007

26KT013

43KT09

32KT132

32KT023

26KT013

12KT040

21KT011

18KT024

26KT013

20KT20

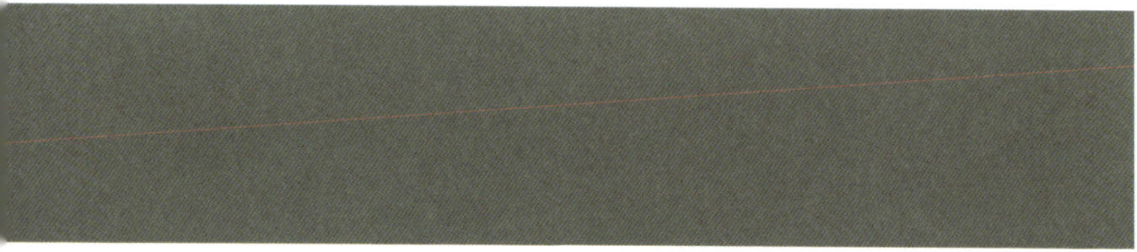

18KT020

43KT12

26KT013

12KT043

32KT132

21KT003

26KT013

18KT016

18KT021

14KT003

26KT013

06KT034

24KT050

26KT015

26KT013

PEARL GRAY

32KT013

32KT029

18KT020

08KT022

32KT013

32KT032

43KT04

43KT02

32KT013

23KT114

24KT026

18KT017

32KT013

32KT123

32KT043

32KT010

32KT013

32KT141

32KT095

32KT033

32KT013

18KT024

11KT114

24KT040

32KT013

17KT004

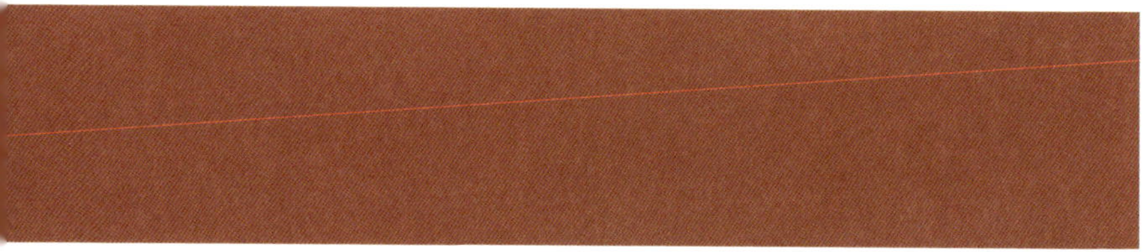

25KT001

21KT011

32KT013

32KT012

26KT073

07KT055

32KT013

32KT014

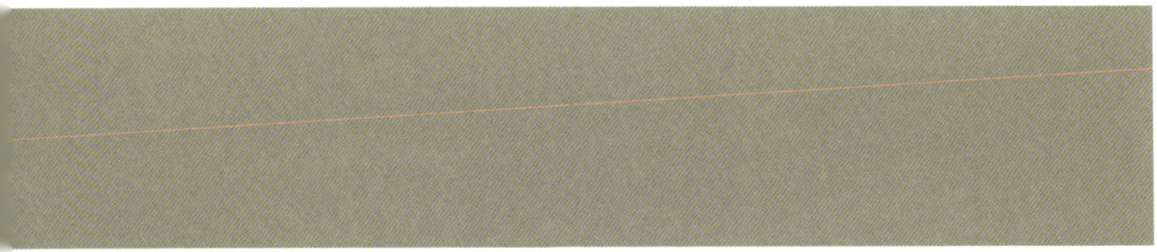

24KT020

12KT043

32KT013

43KT10

06KT001

17KT036

32KT013

DUSKY GRAY

16KT002

14KT050

23KT114

24KT090

16KT002

32KT023

32KT109

43KT02

16KT002

24KT090

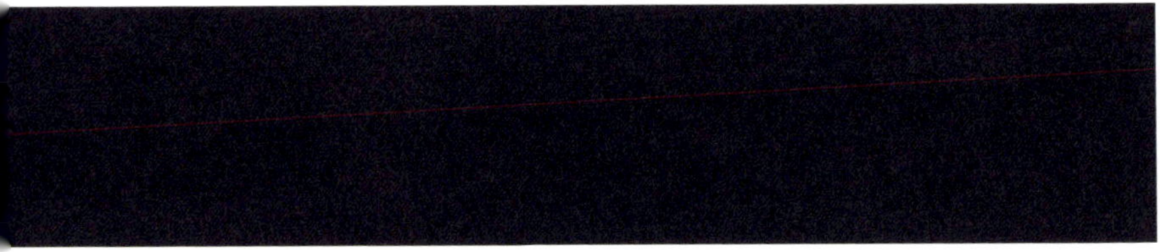

12KT048

16KT003

16KT002

04KT004

43KT23

16KT001

16KT002

21KT001

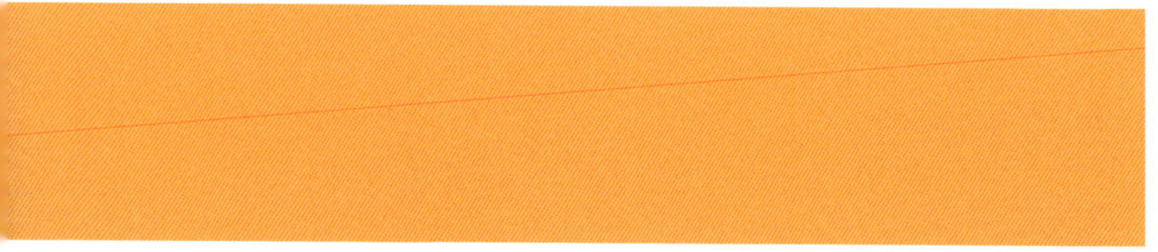

43KT22

43KT18

16KT002

18KT016

21KT005

21KT002

16KT002

14KT003

12KT001

11KT114

16KT002

32KT043

11KT020

12KT099

16KT002

20KT20

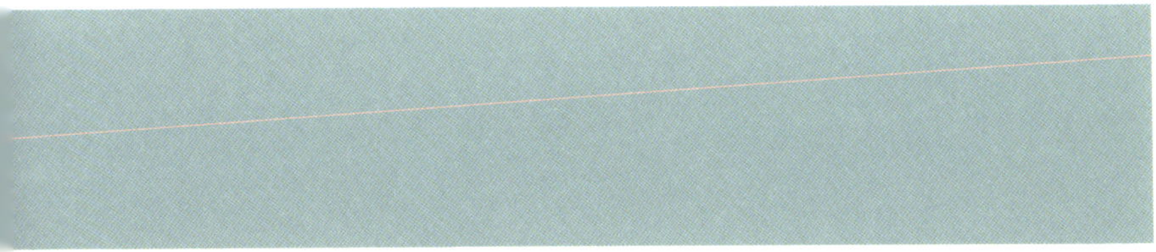

32KT032

43KT06

16KT002

12KT040

07KT015

17KT036

16KT002

PALE NATIVE UMBER

32KT143

32KT023

32KT110

32KT140

32KT143

12KT044

08KT009

26KT012

32KT143

32KT021

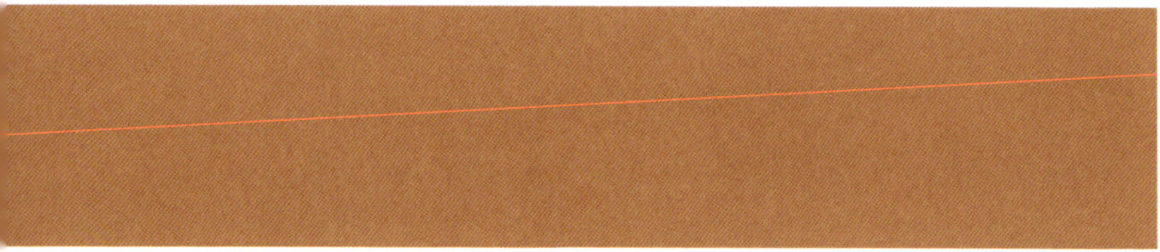

12KT121

32KT014

32KT143

26KT046

26KT071

16KT061

32KT143

43KT01

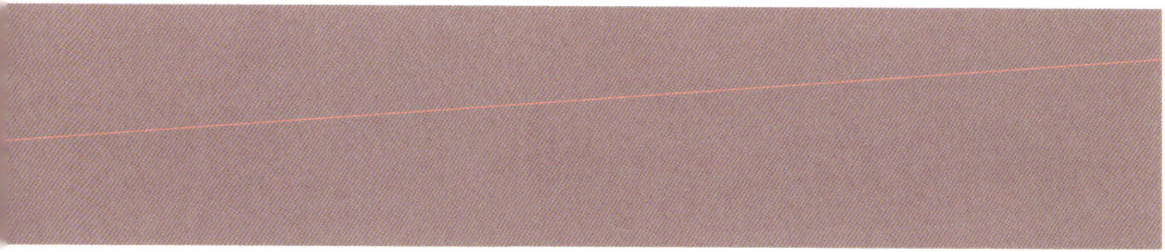

08KT008

32KT012

32KT143

21KT003

24KT041

06KT034

32KT143

18KT018

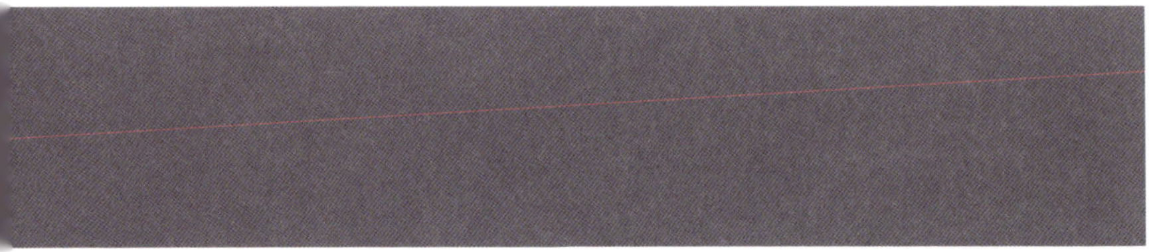

21KT006

32KT142

32KT143

32KT141

26KT040

26KT072

32KT143

21KT012

20KT318

21KT011

32KT143

24KT094

43KT17

09KT024

32KT143

SANDY UMBER

11KT054

21KT013

18KT026

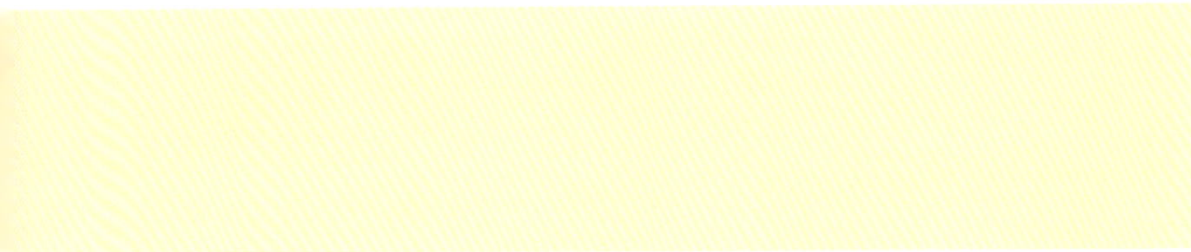

18KT024

11KT054

43KT05

32KT029

21KT007

11KT054

18KT025

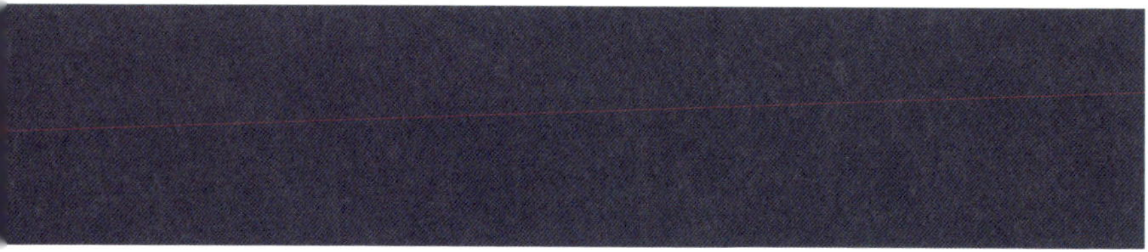

11KT092

32KT033

11KT054

10KT010

43KT26

16KT006

11KT054

12KT056

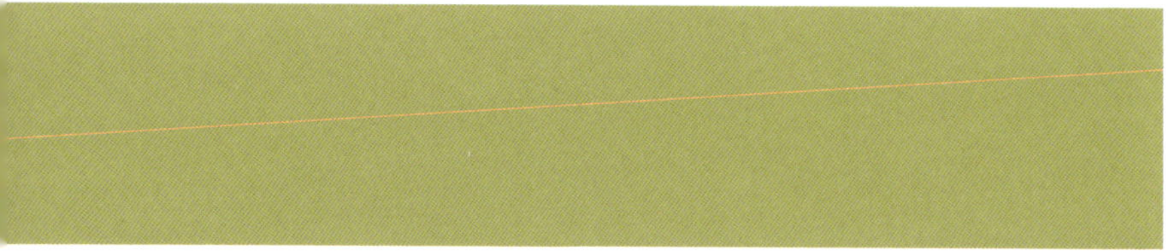

11KT115

16KT005

11KT054

43KT09

32KT033

32KT109

11KT054

23KT020

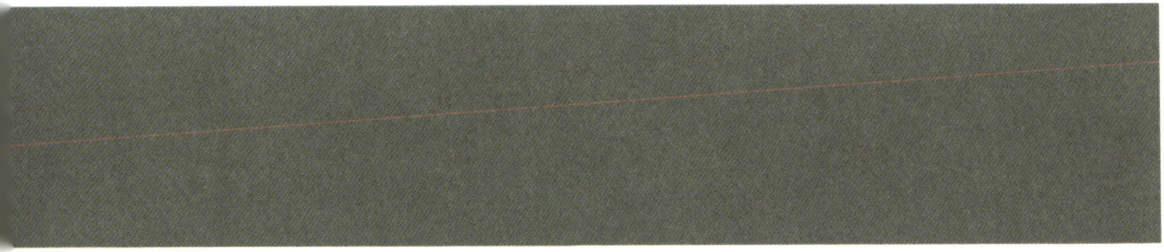

18KT020

12KT043

11KT054

08KT001

22KT021

21KT014

11KT054

32KT095

21KT009

43KT19

11KT054

10KT001

24KT040

08KT007

11KT054

SANDSTONE

21KT004

26KT015

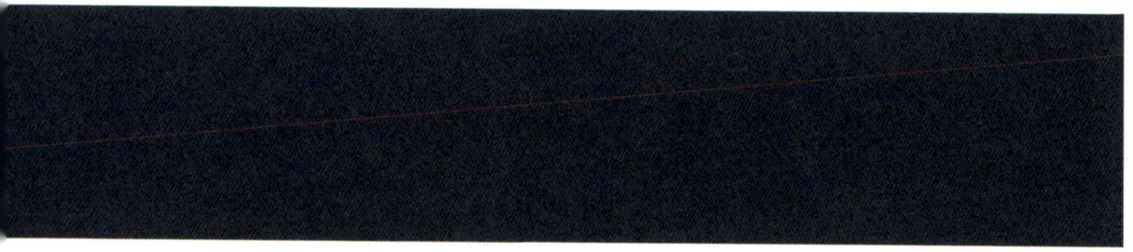

13KT023

17KT059

21KT004

22KT034

25KT001

18KT014

21KT004

18KT021

18KT022

43KT12

21KT004

21KT013

12KT001

11KT120

21KT004

10KT075

07KT055

24KT020

21KT004

04KT003

32KT110

32KT024

21KT004

13KT095

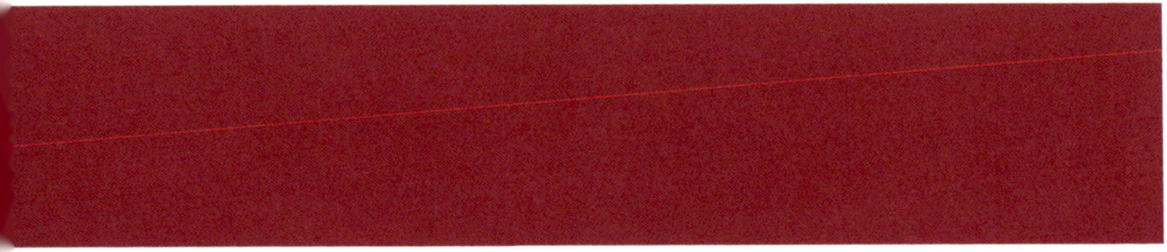

32KT101

08KT006

21KT004

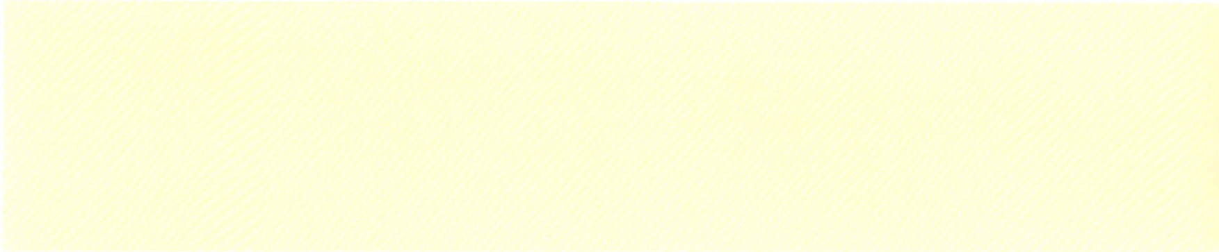

07KT056

20KT305

24KT050

21KT004

43KT11

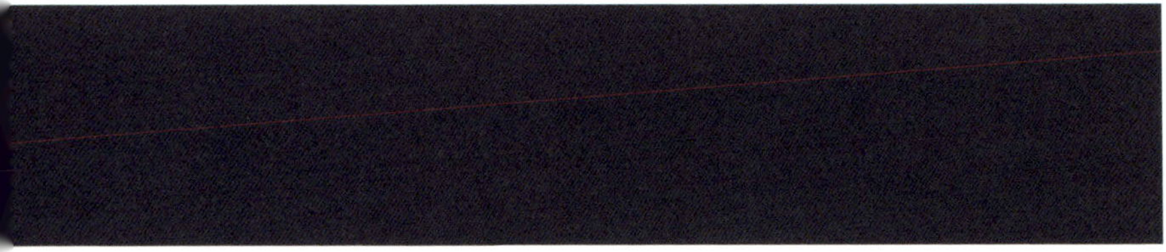

10KT003

32KT034

21KT004

32KT007

07KT015

06KT001

21KT004

LIGHT NATIVE UMBER

32KT142

12KT099

43KT04

20KT305

32KT142

22KT034

11KT114

18KT017

32KT142

32KT014

06KT001

32KT141

32KT142

14KT050

18KT016

32KT024

32KT142

13KT095

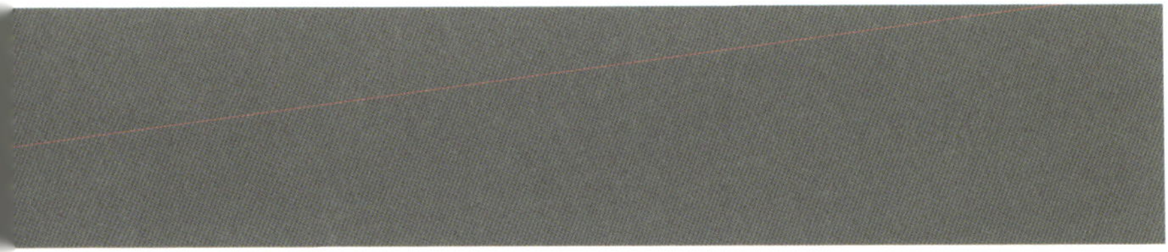

21KT011

25KT001

32KT142

08KT009

32KT022

23KT114

32KT142

08KT003

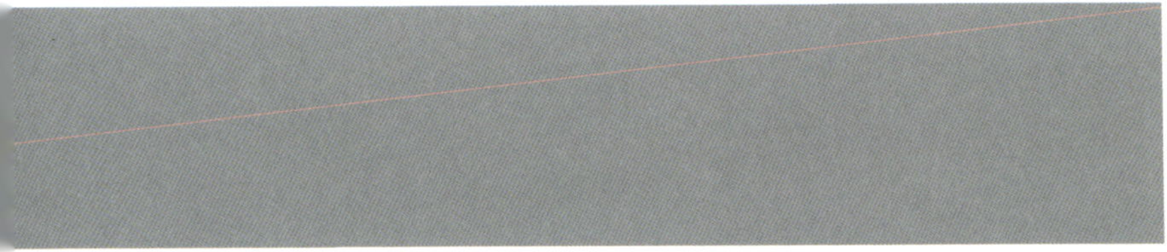

18KT027

18KT016

32KT142

32KT029

18KT020

12KT043

32KT142

14KT003

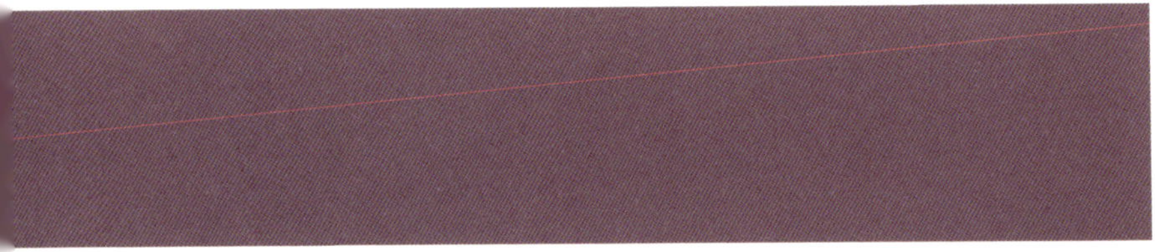

07KT055

12KT121

32KT142

04KT003

22KT021

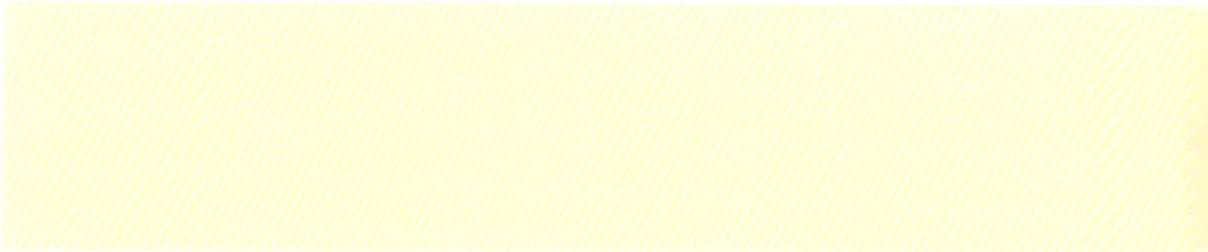

07KT056

32KT142

HOUSE BY THE SEA

17KT004

32KT110

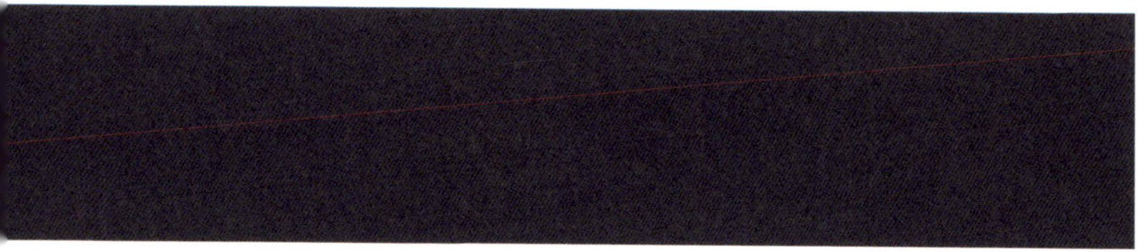

10KT003

17KT059

17KT004

20KT318

18KT022

18KT021

17KT004

15KT057

12KT044

21KT006

17KT004

43KT23

18KT020

16KT006

17KT004

12KT056

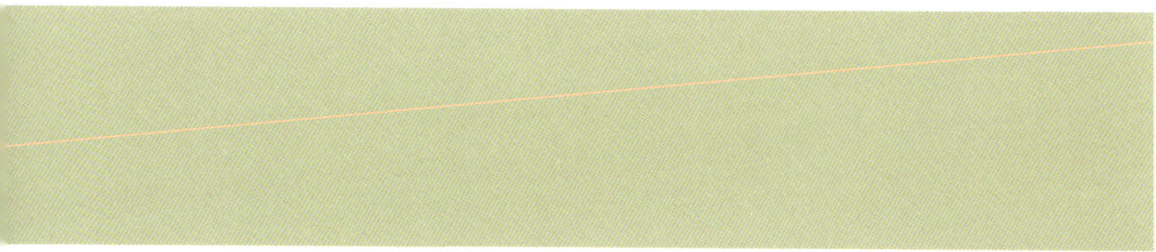

26KT046

32KT023

17KT004

16KT006

12KT048

11KT114

17KT004

17KT060

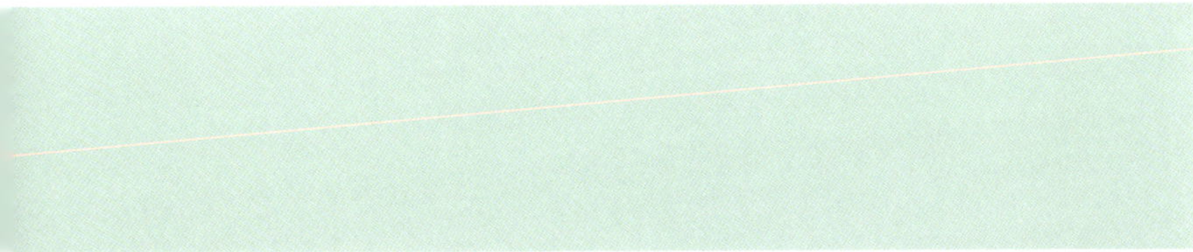

32KT034

11KT020

17KT004

18KT028

08KT009

22KT021

17KT004

32KT032

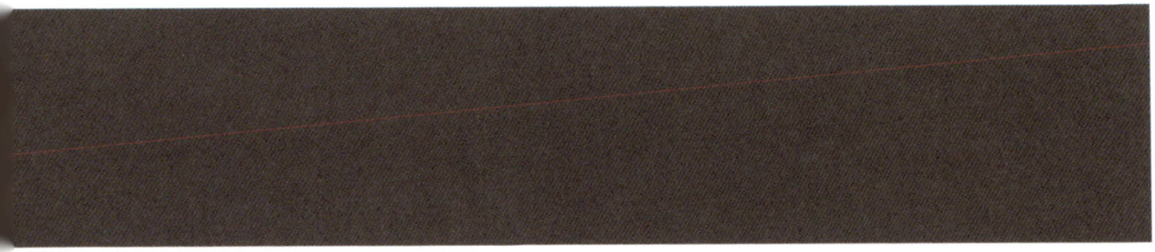

43KT16

43KT12

17KT004

11KT120

13KT023

32KT131

17KT004

CYPRUS UMBER 272 PALE

08KT005

32KT010

21KT014

09KT024

08KT005

43KT09

18KT021

11KT114

08KT005

08KT006

32KT041

32KT110

08KT005

08KT007

10KT001

06KT034

08KT005

43KT22

10KT001

08KT006

08KT005

21KT001

43KT05

11KT115

08KT005

32KT109

12KT056

18KT014

08KT005

08KT001

07KT055

16KT001

08KT005

12KT050

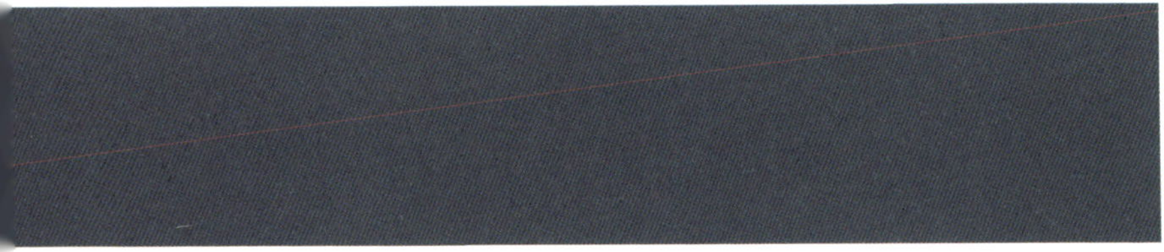

22KT034

12KT121

08KT005

12KT043

17KT036

21KT002

08KT005

PALE BURNT UMBER

08KT013

32KT034

04KT004

32KT010

08KT013

32KT029

15KT057

11KT020

08KT013

43KT02

26KT046

12KT052

08KT013

13KT009

43KT26

17KT060

08KT013

15KT057

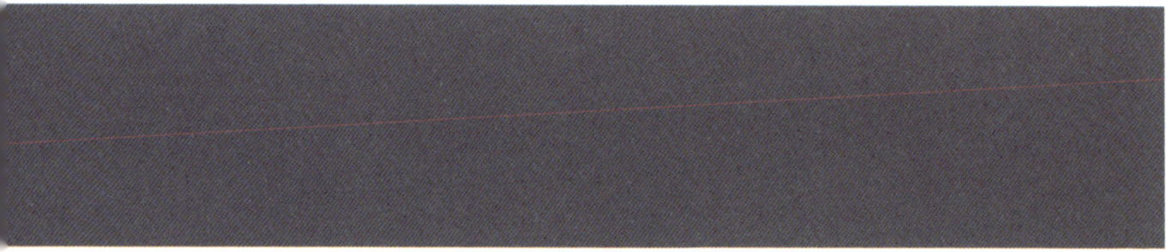

16KT061

32KT100

08KT013

13KT095

12KT056

18KT027

08KT013

15KT057

16KT001

43KT04

08KT013

12KT046

32KT131

20KT305

08KT013

32KT012

32KT041

09KT024

08KT013

43KT04

17KT059

13KT023

08KT013

ART GALLERY GRAY

26KT012

32KT095

32KT024

21KT012

26KT012

20KT305

32KT140

26KT013

26KT012

32KT141

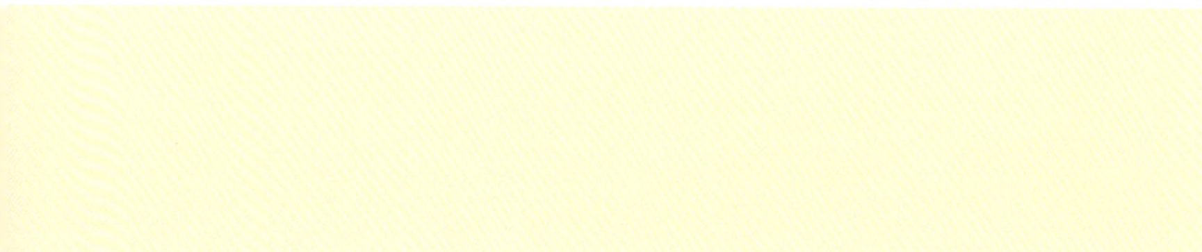

18KT024

11KT092

26KT012

32KT109

21KT012

24KT091

26KT012

16KT001

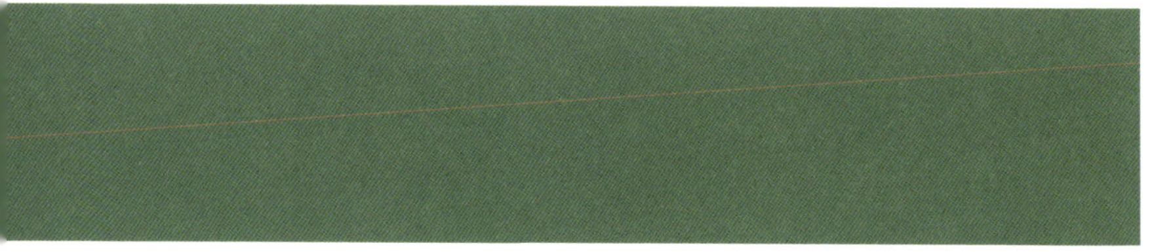

24KT041

32KT023

26KT012

32KT110

20KT305

26KT015

26KT012

10KT010

43KT04

08KT044

26KT012

11KT092

25KT001

14KT003

26KT012

08KT009

32KT123

32KT006

26KT012

43KT11

26KT015

26KT013

26KT012

LIMESTONE GRAY

21KT002

17KT036

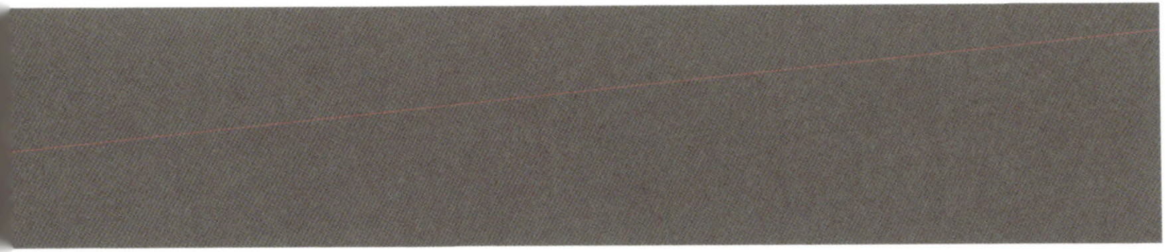

32KT010

32KT110

21KT002

07KT015

22KT034

21KT005

21KT002

08KT044

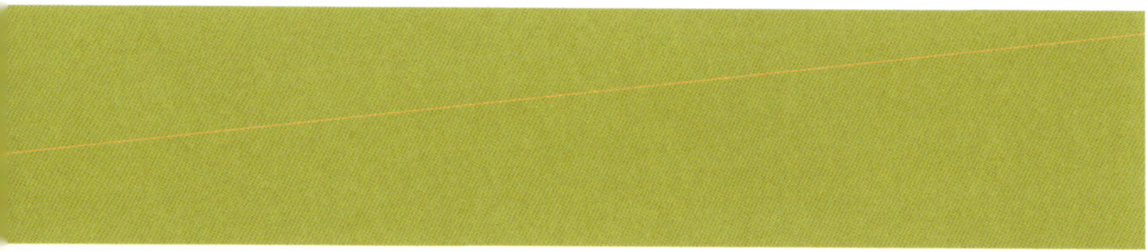

43KT06

32KT140

21KT002

43KT17

32KT041

32KT034

21KT002

32KT014

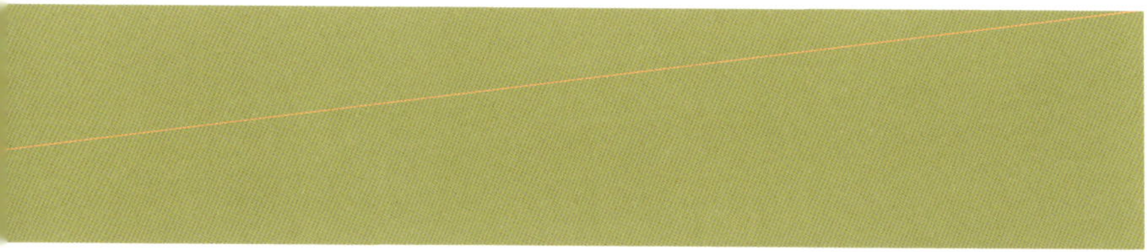

11KT115

04KT004

21KT002

32KT032

43KT09

12KT121

21KT002

43KT16

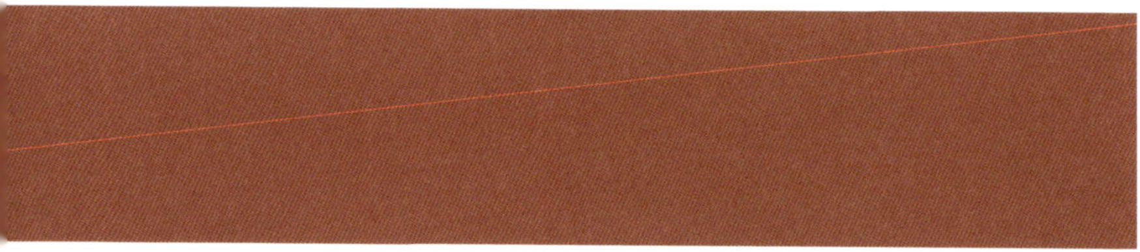

25KT001

32KT033

21KT002

24KT091

16KT006

16KT005

21KT002

24KT050

32KT032

43KT22

21KT002

12KT001

08KT009

16KT006

21KT002

SHALE GRAY

16KT001

06KT034

32KT041

11KT114

16KT001

08KT008

12KT040

43KT04

16KT001

16KT003

43KT26

25KT001

16KT001

16KT002

07KT055

24KT041

16KT001

43KT06

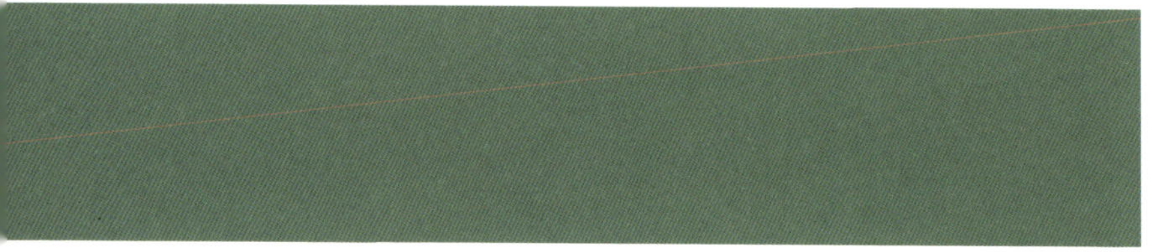

24KT041

26KT073

16KT001

18KT018

21KT005

04KT003

16KT001

43KT18

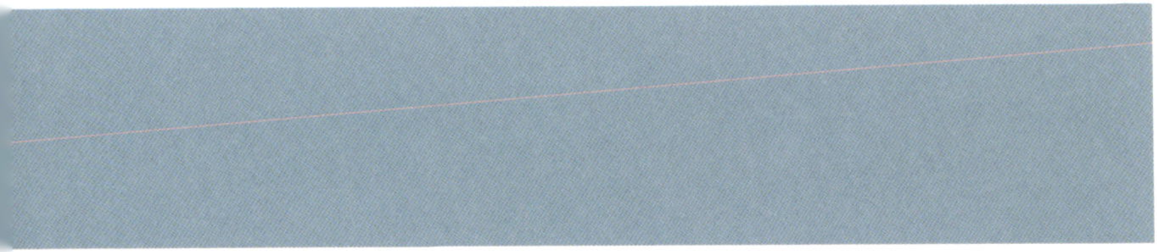

32KT031

32KT110

16KT001

10KT003

32KT102

23KT114

16KT001

20KT20

24KT040

17KT059

16KT001

32KT034

43KT26

43KT05

16KT001

MEDIUM NATIVE UMBER

32KT141

13KT095

12KT043

10KT001

32KT141

22KT022

20KT305

26KT046

32KT141

24KT026

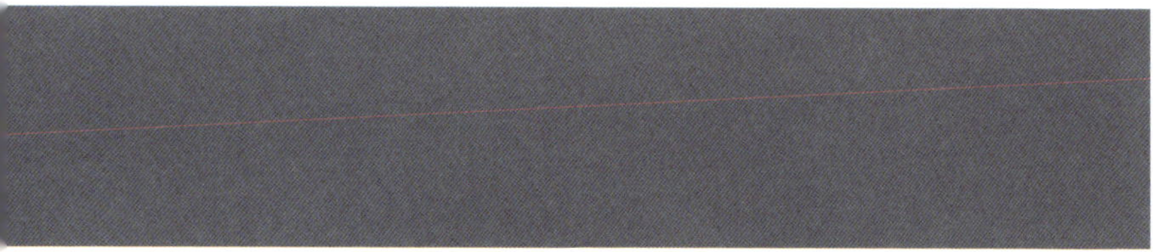

22KT021

12KT121

32KT141

21KT013

11KT120

32KT024

32KT141

17KT036

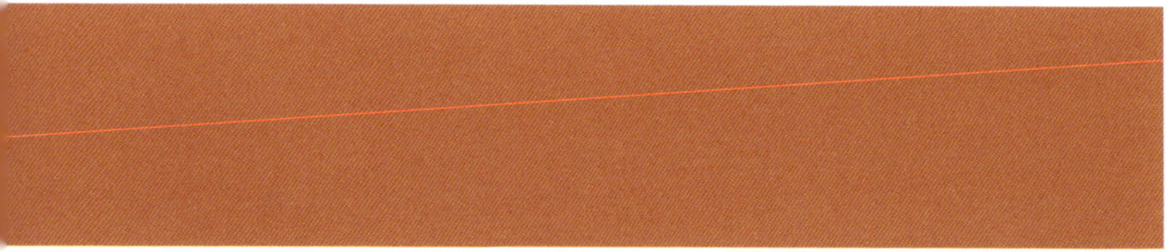

43KT23

04KT004

32KT141

32KT143

10KT001

43KT06

32KT141

12KT057

10KT001

43KT04

32KT141

23KT114

21KT014

24KT026

32KT141

32KT101

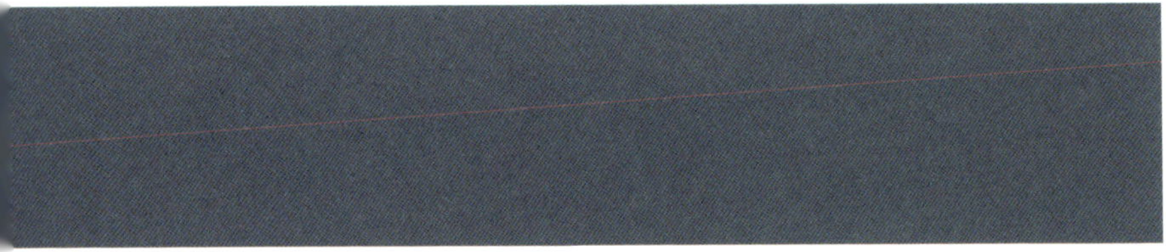

22KT034

32KT102

32KT141

18KT025

20KT305

11KT092

32KT141

NOVEMBER GRAY

21KT001

18KT024

32KT042

32KT033

21KT001

43KT02

21KT010

08KT009

21KT001

32KT014

32KT123

16KT005

21KT001

26KT015

20KT318

08KT003

21KT001

08KT003

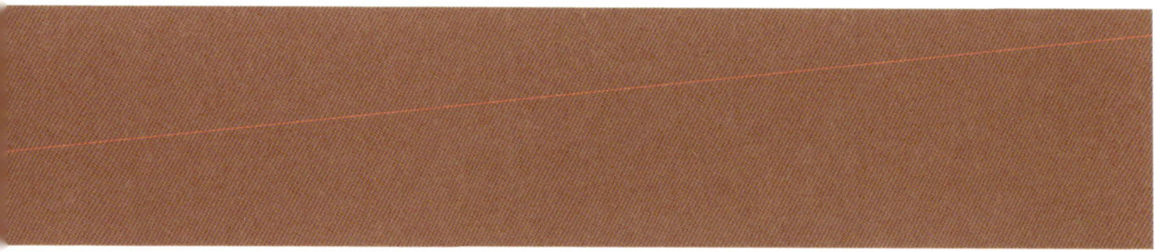

32KT110

08KT006

21KT001

21KT009

12KT043

13KT095

21KT001

13KT095

14KT003

18KT021

21KT001

32KT034

16KT002

22KT022

21KT001

21KT013

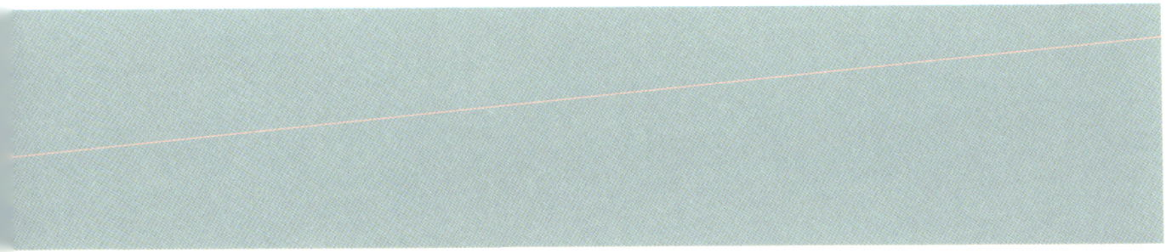

32KT032

23KT114

21KT001

26KT046

16KT006

21KT004

21KT001

UMBER GRAY

14KT050

23KT020

43KT26

18KT017

14KT050

26KT073

21KT012

21KT004

14KT050

22KT021

17KT004

25KT001

14KT050

43KT04

17KT059

23KT020

14KT050

32KT110

24KT026

32KT034

14KT050

18KT020

18KT022

32KT132

14KT050

10KT075

10KT001

18KT021

14KT050

08KT003

21KT006

08KT001

14KT050

43KT05

16KT002

26KT073

14KT050

06KT034

24KT040

17KT004

14KT050

IRON GRAY

32KT010

09KT024

11KT054

32KT014

32KT010

21KT013

32KT123

32KT014

32KT010

32KT014

21KT012

32KT095

32KT010

25KT001

21KT012

08KT013

32KT010

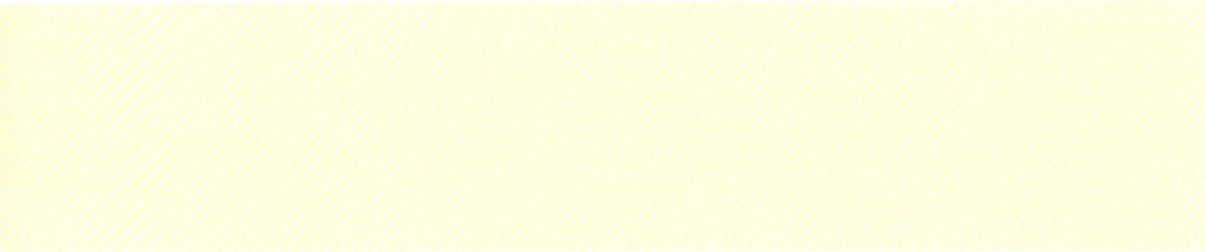

18KT024

43KT12

21KT009

32KT010

18KT016

18KT026

32KT014

32KT010

22KT034

12KT099

32KT131

32KT010

08KT006

32KT109

21KT013

32KT010

32KT014

32KT033

16KT005

32KT010

32KT006

32KT011

24KT090

32KT010

MINERAL GRAY

24KT050

32KT007

17KT059

24KT094

24KT050

32KT041

32KT023

26KT012

24KT050

17KT060

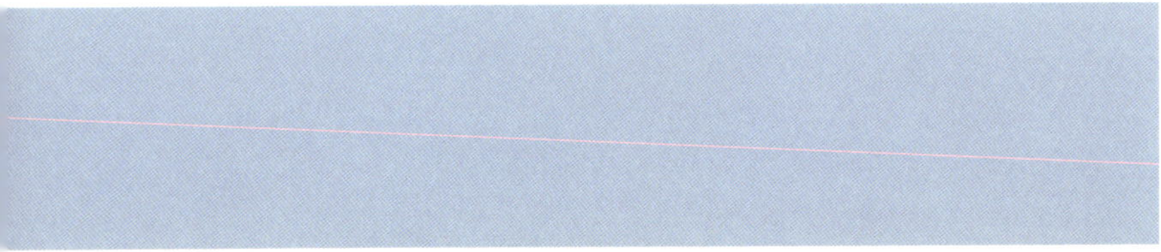

13KT009

18KT026

24KT050

15KT057

32KT024

21KT011

24KT050

32KT021

43KT17

11KT115

24KT050

32KT042

18KT028

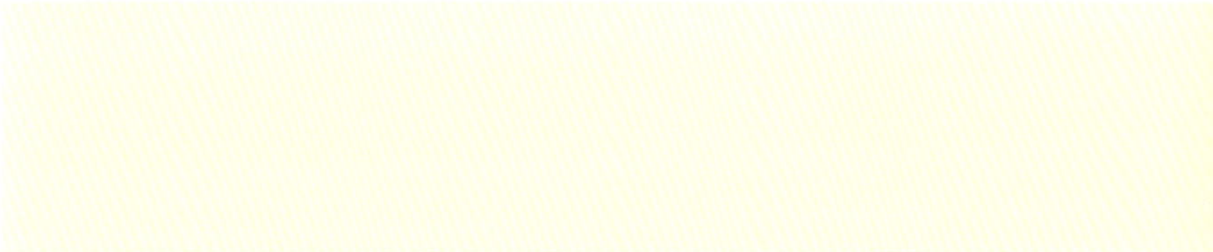

08KT001

24KT050

24KT090

21KT010

11KT120

24KT050

21KT014

43KT23

12KT099

24KT050

07KT055

07KT056

16KT002

24KT050

18KT017

16KT061

15KT057

24KT050

ANTHRACITE

10KT010

06KT001

07KT056

32KT012

10KT010

21KT012

25KT001

26KT015

10KT010

08KT001

08KT044

43KT12

10KT010

17KT059

15KT057

24KT040

10KT010

32KT006

12KT057

21KT006

10KT010

14KT003

11KT092

16KT003

10KT010

32KT012

26KT046

24KT090

10KT010

43KT12

32KT013

43KT02

10KT010

14KT003

12KT001

21KT013

10KT010

43KT11

18KT021

32KT022

10KT010

DARK NATIVE UMBER

32KT140

21KT014

32KT109

20KT20

32KT140

32KT023

32KT011

23KT114

32KT140

16KT061

13KT095

06KT034

32KT140

17KT060

12KT099

20KT305

32KT140

32KT006

32KT109

07KT015

32KT140

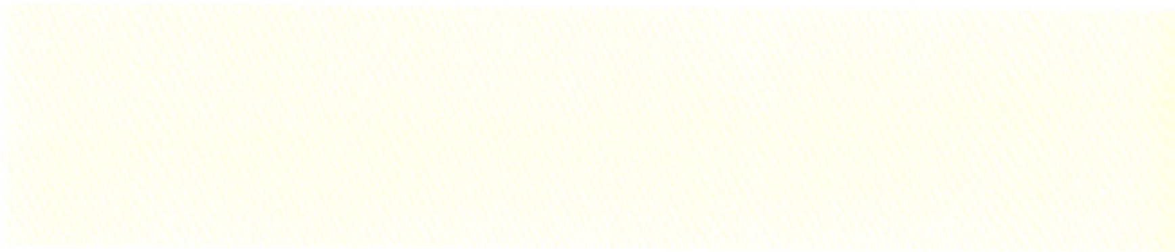

08KT001

11KT114

18KT017

32KT140

18KT014

32KT029

43KT23

32KT140

18KT028

32KT123

18KT027

32KT140

43KT12

32KT142

43KT02

32KT140

12KT044

18KT028

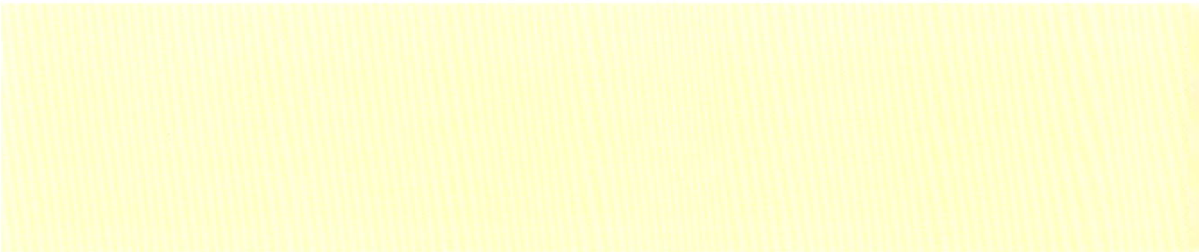

07KT056

32KT140

CHESTNUT BROWN

32KT130

32KT032

18KT016

32KT132

32KT130

17KT004

18KT020

21KT009

32KT130

21KT013

24KT090

24KT091

32KT130

21KT001

21KT014

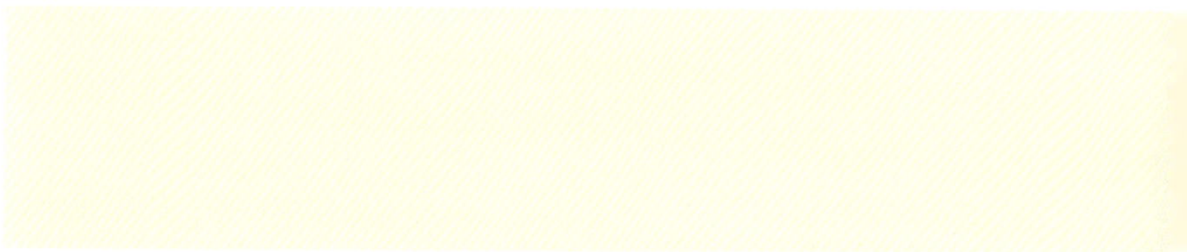

10KT075

32KT130

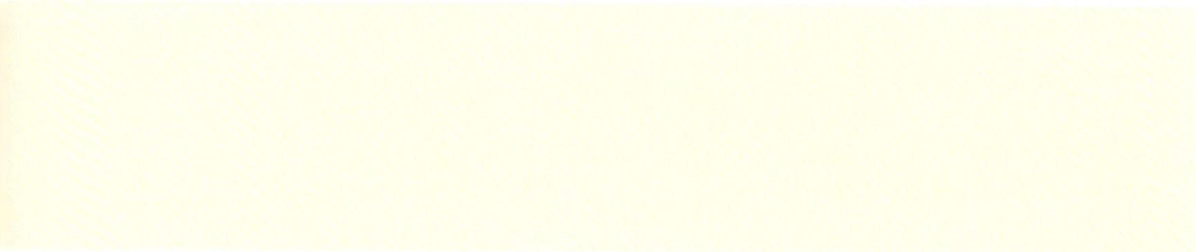

08KT001

32KT095

32KT023

32KT130

32KT110

21KT012

32KT006

32KT130

43KT19

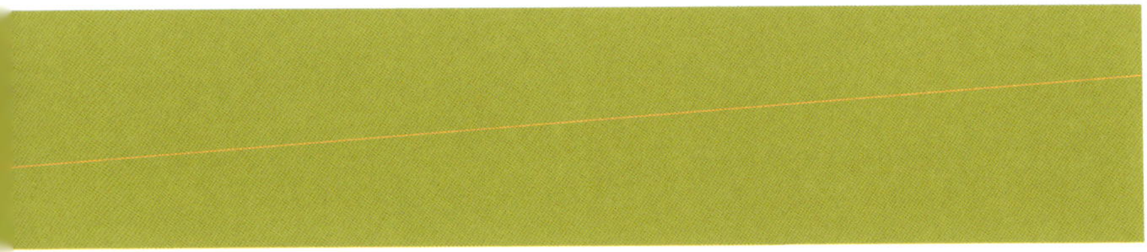

43KT06

16KT003

32KT130

18KT028

12KT099

08KT009

32KT130

23KT114

21KT010

20KT20

32KT130

26KT046

32KT141

20KT305

32KT130

PALE NATURAL SIENNA

26KT073

32KT140

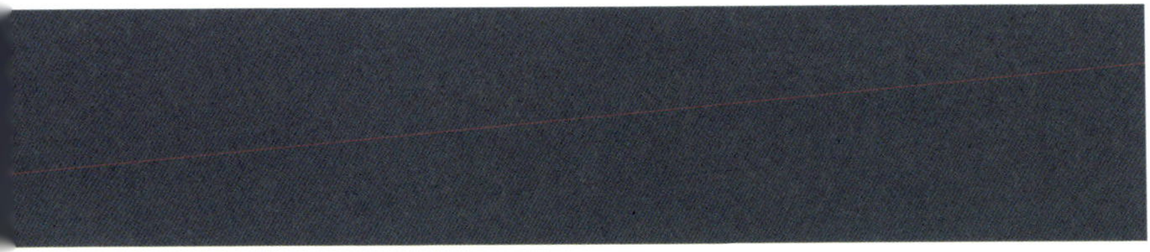

22KT034

32KT042

26KT073

18KT015

12KT043

18KT022

26KT073

13KT009

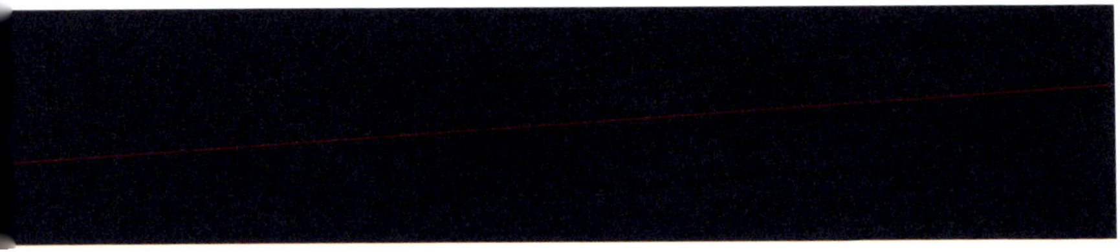

04KT003

32KT141

26KT073

17KT059

17KT060

11KT020

26KT073

12KT044

17KT060

32KT006

26KT073

13KT095

08KT044

09KT024

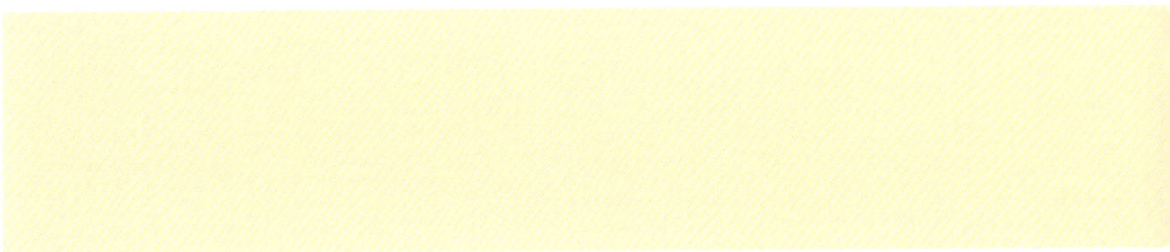

26KT073

18KT022

18KT020

12KT099

26KT073

32KT042

24KT040

08KT006

26KT073

24KT020

10KT001

08KT003

26KT073

32KT014

12KT043

21KT013

26KT073

LIGHT NATURAL SIENNA

26KT072

32KT140

26KT040

18KT017

26KT072

43KT23

43KT09

32KT024

26KT072

32KT042

32KT095

24KT050

26KT072

21KT001

18KT021

12KT099

26KT072

08KT005

21KT003

21KT009

26KT072

32KT024

32KT043

12KT052

26KT072

32KT109

43KT19

32KT006

26KT072

08KT001

21KT002

21KT010

26KT072

11KT115

32KT140

07KT055

26KT072

18KT028

16KT005

12KT121

26KT072

LIGHT SAHARA SAND

09KT003

12KT050

16KT006

16KT003

09KT003

32KT034

32KT032

43KT17

09KT003

21KT002

43KT26

21KT010

09KT003

22KT021

32KT014

32KT142

09KT003

11KT120

08KT009

12KT056

09KT003

12KT057

18KT014

18KT015

09KT003

24KT020

32KT014

12KT046

09KT003

13KT023

32KT110

17KT060

09KT003

32KT011

43KT12

32KT022

09KT003

14KT050

43KT23

23KT020

09KT003

MEDIUM NATURAL SIENNA

26KT071

13KT095

21KT006

21KT014

26KT071

20KT20

32KT023

32KT010

26KT071

24KT041

43KT17

21KT005

26KT071

26KT073

43KT01

32KT033

26KT071

24KT040

08KT009

21KT003

26KT071

25KT001

22KT021

21KT014

26KT071

07KT055

11KT115

11KT092

26KT071

16KT003

13KT009

16KT001

26KT071

43KT23

18KT020

10KT003

26KT071

26KT012

26KT015

06KT001

26KT071

SAHARA SAND

09KT002

07KT056

32KT012

10KT001

09KT002

22KT021

17KT004

12KT044

09KT002

16KT002

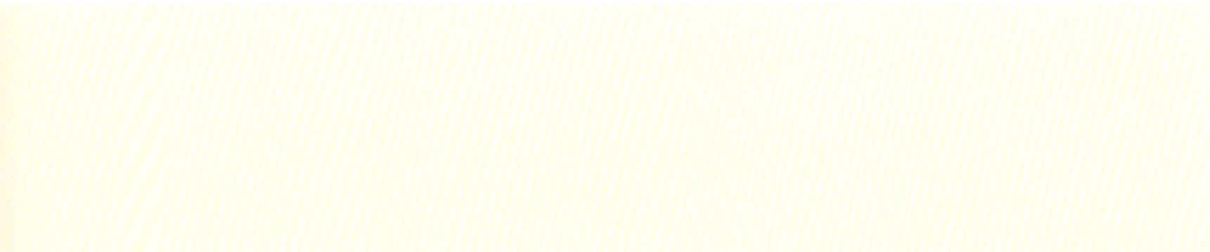

08KT001

18KT016

09KT002

26KT015

32KT100

21KT001

09KT002

12KT048

43KT26

20KT20

09KT002

08KT006

26KT040

32KT006

09KT002

04KT004

43KT04

12KT056

09KT002

23KT114

18KT027

18KT017

09KT002

21KT010

32KT140

26KT040

09KT002

16KT061

12KT099

43KT04

09KT002

COLOR INDEX

COLOR	COLOR VALUE	PAGE
04KT003 Prussian Blue *Pariserblau*	RGB 025 026 033 CMYK 84 75 56 77	29, 118, 161, 241, 257, 325, 430
04KT004 Ultramarine Cobalt Green *Ultramarinkobaltgrün*	RGB 000 117 143 CMYK 91 42 37 02	48, 135, 203, 284, 312, 336, 482
06KT001 Hot Magenta *Hot Magenta*	RGB 180 019 119 CMYK 32 100 11 00	33, 171, 197, 245, 250, 392, 473
06KT034 Green Tea *Grüner Tee*	RGB 219 221 145 CMYK 19 04 54 00	47, 88, 113, 185, 217, 275, 320, 365, 406
07KT015 Veronese Green *Vert Véronèse foncé*	RGB 134 144 120 CMYK 49 30 52 15	32, 82, 169, 176, 209, 245, 309, 408
07KT055 Loos' Violet *Loos Violett*	RGB 131 085 120 CMYK 53 71 29 13	15, 50, 105, 121, 168, 172, 195, 240, 256, 279, 323, 388, 448, 470

INDEX

INDEX

INDEX

INDEX

INDEX

INDEX

PAGE	COLOR VALUE	COLOR
37, 72, 83, 99, 106, 188ff, 399	RGB 192 194 196 CMYK 28 20 20 02	**32KT013** Pearl Gray *Gris perle*
68ff, 196, 214, 250, 312, 346, 368, 369, 370, 373, 376, 437, 455, 458	RGB 232 227 224 CMYK 10 10 11 01	**32KT014** Natural Gray *Gris natur*
142, 214, 384	RGB 144 179 218 CMYK 48 22 04 00	**32KT021** Sky Blue *Bleu ciel*
86, 106, 136, 253, 401, 460	RGB 166 188 211 CMYK 40 20 11 00	**32KT022** Medium Ultramarine Blue *Bleu outremer moyen*
27, 59, 81, 84, 149, 180, 201, 212, 264, 300, 381, 405, 420, 465	RGB 182 199 218 CMYK 33 16 10 00	**32KT023** Light Blue *Bleu clair*
241, 251, 296, 335, 383, 441, 445	RGB 220 225 229 CMYK 15 08 08 02	**32KT024** Pale Blue *Bleu pâle*
179, 188, 225, 255, 285, 410	RGB 243 247 250 CMYK 06 02 02 00	**32KT029** Lapis Lazuli White *Lapislazuliweiß*
46, 326	RGB 120 163 189 CMYK 57 25 18 02	**32KT031** Bright Cerulean Blue *Bleu ceruleum vif*
12, 39, 146, 158, 189, 208, 268, 313, 316, 352, 416, 453	RGB 156 188 207 CMYK 44 16 17 01	**32KT032** Medium Cerulean Blue 2 *Bleu ceruleum moyen 2*

INDEX

INDEX